Christmas Nights

Miranda Maynard

This edition first published in paperback by
Michael Terence Publishing in 2022
www.mtp.agency

Copyright © 2022 Miranda Maynard

Miranda Maynard has asserted the right to be identified as
the author of this work in accordance with the
Copyright, Designs and Patents Act 1988

ISBN 9781800944770

No part of this publication may be reproduced, stored
in a retrieval system, or transmitted, in any form or
by any means, electronic, mechanical, photocopying,
recording or otherwise, without the prior
permission of the publisher

Cover image
Copyright © Jenny Ateua
www.123rf.com

Cover design
Copyright © 2022 Michael Terence Publishing

Contents

Chapter 1:
Days Leading to Christmas 1

Chapter 2:
The Mystique 7

Chapter 3:
Christmas Films 9

Chapter 4:
Christmas Day 13

Chapter 5:
Boxing Day 15

Chapter 6:
On a Christmas Morning 17

Invitation to the Family 19

New Year's Celebration 21

Footnote 23

Chapter 1:

Days Leading to Christmas

Michael helped his Mother put up the Christmas decorations on a Christmas Tree. The natural Christmas Tree looked lovely with Christmas decorations, tinsel and with flashing Christmas lights which came on and off. In the dark, the Christmas lights shone. In the glowing light, it was an electrifying enchantment.

Michael, a teenager, stood by a Christmas Tree and looked at the tinsel covering the whole tree. The tinsel glittered in the shining light.

Michael admired the really beautiful Christmas Tree. Michael dreamt about Christmas. He dreamt of a white Christmas. It was quite unlikely it would snow at Christmas.

Michael dreamed that his Father would come and see him (Michael's Father was divorced and his son felt deserted and abandoned).

Michael looked forward to Christmas. He had a childish perspective of Christmas. He became really excited at the prospect of Christmas. His seasonal joy was a boy's excitement. The Christmas season was thrilling.

"Son, are you looking forward to Christmas?" asked Mother.

"Oh! Yes. I am. It's a pity Father won't be here," replied son.

Jenny held her son in her arms. Comforting her son with affection.

"Son, you have me."

The emotional son was deeply upset. Michael suppressed his tears. In the lounge, Michael sat in an armchair in front of the fire (place).

Michael took such comfort from being comfortable. Michael thought of his Father. Michael greatly missed his Father. He felt so deeply sad especially about his Father's intentional absence this Christmas.

Michael relaxed by the fire. Keeping himself warm.

The lounge was filled with seasonal Christmas decorations. All over the big room, there were Christmas cards everywhere. Covering the edges of all the frames of paintings and pictures hung tinsel which glittered. These pictures and paintings hanging on the wall were covered with tinsel.

Michael got up. He came out into the garden. There he found his sister Angela with her school friends. His sister Angela invited the three of them to her house. One of the older girls looked very pretty wearing a dress and the other two girls with good looks were casually dressed.

Michael met them. These teenage strangers. Then all of a sudden, his sister and her three so-called friends left the house. Michael never saw any of Angela's friends ever again.

During the next morning at Christmastime, Michael watched the Detective Season. A black and white film. It was nostalgic. Afterwards, Michael went to his bedroom to lie down and rest. Coming downstairs, he joined his Mother. His Mother sat in an armchair and flicked through a magazine.

"Your sister is not here. You're here with me," said Mother.

"Christmas can be a misery. Not everybody has a happy Christmas. Do they?" said son.

Jenny spoke about the certain significance of Christmas.

"Christmas is a seasonal celebration. Isn't it for love, harmony and peace and goodwill to men?"

"Isn't it in the stable? That's the religious aspect of it? It's biblical," said son.

"That's the true meaning of Christmas. Do you believe?"

Michael remained sceptical about it.

"I dare say I do. I don't understand."

"How many times have I drummed it into you, for you to say your prayers and to go to church," scolded Mother.

"I don't believe."

"Michael, I have taught you to read your bible. Why have you stopped doing it?"

"Mom. I don't believe," said son sceptically.

Jenny ripped open the cellophane on a box of chocolates and passed it to her son. Michael reached out and took a chocolate. A chocolate nutty almond. Jenny was inclined to be peaceable at Christmastime. Especially towards her son.

Usually, Michael felt unhappy, miserable, tense and worried. In his present state of mind, he felt peaceful, cheerful, calm and relaxed. Enjoying the peace and quiet of Christmas. The son and Mother, having a good relationship, enjoyed the company of one another. Despite it being a broken family. A single-parent family.

Michael appeared philosophically conversational.

"Christmas coming is bliss and joy. Will we ever find true happiness? Christmas is a time when families gather together and celebrate Christmas. Why is it, in our case, it is not happening? What's wrong with this delinquent family?" frowned son.

"Son, I don't know. Your guess is as good as mine."

As his Mother got up to make a cup of tea, Michael stepped outside of the house. He shivered in the cold weather. Tonight, it was a cold Christmas night. The glory of Christmas was truly wonderful!

All alone with his Mother, it was a pleasurable joy. Such a glorious peace.

Christmas nights and days. A thrilling, electrifying sensation of the gloriousness of this Christmas Night.

Going back indoors. Michael relaxed with his Mother. Both of them enjoyed having a cup of tea. They both engaged in conversation.

That Christmas night they both cherished and enjoyed the peace and quiet of Christmas. This Christmas night was beautiful and peaceful.

Actually, for Michael being in the presence of his Mother remained quite a pleasant experience. It was something precious that he would remember in his lifetime.

"Things have changed in life. Now there is no more quarrelling anymore. There is peace at last. It is peace at Xmas," said son cheerfully.

"Your Father has married. He has his own life now," said Mother calmly.

"Mum it's just you and me."

Jenny got up and walked to the other side where another armchair faced opposite, on the other side near the suite. Jenny moving to her son had put her arm around him. Feeling passionate emotion Jenny comforted her son. Jenny consoled her son. "My Boy!"

Chapter 2:

The Mystique

Michael and his Mother came to a Birthday party. Mrs Pollock's Daughter's birthday party. The semi-detached house was situated near a railway line.

Mrs Pollock welcomed Jenny and Michael. There inside the house were Gillian's friends invited to her Birthday party.

Michael met teenage strangers. They were mostly females, Gillian's friends. None of the guests there paid any attention to him. The room Michael entered was empty. Meanwhile, Michael's Mother spent time with Mrs Pollock, a monstrosity.

In a spacious wooden room, strange music played. There, many Teenagers danced together. To his surprise, Michael saw a strange Teenage Blonde Girl dancing there. A mystique, galaxy. The Girl, an enigma wore a beautiful evening dress. Her back was exposed.

Michael was charmed by the mysterious Girl's sweet smile. The dancing girl was an enigma!

Michael desired her. The Blonde looked alluring and enticing. The girl was irresistible. Michael danced close to her. He smelled the scent of her beautiful perfume. Her perspiration.

They danced next to each other. They both wooed each other. The girl's hair touched him.

Suddenly a Teenage boy insulted him. Michael was unafraid of the provocative insulter. Michael kept his composure and continued dancing with the mystique.

As soon as the music stopped and the dance ended, the Blonde's close friend entered the room holding a silver platter of drumsticks.

Michael became bewitched by the sight of all the strangers there. The strangers he met were a fleeting encounter. Suddenly, Gillian's plump Mother burst into the room. Fran raising her voice ordered everybody to leave now.

"The party has ended. NOW GO!"

All of Gillian's Birthday Guests obeyed and departed.

Subsequently, Michael and his Mother ended up spending the night at Fran's house.

Leaving early the next morning, Michael and his Mother commuted to get back home. Michael had forgotten to take his pullover which he had inadvertently left behind on a bedroom chair.

Chapter 3:
Christmas Films

The next morning Michael watched television alone. He watched a nostalgic film. It was an old black and white film. The investigation of a sleuth who solved a crime. Michael was engrossed in watching it. He enjoyed watching the mystery.

In the meantime, his Mother, Jenny, came downstairs and went into the kitchen. Jenny did food preparation. Jenny seasoned and marinated the pieces of fish in a baking tray.

After the film ended, Michael went back to his bedroom. That early morning Michael got in his bed. In his bed, he rested for hours.

Hours later, Michael came back downstairs to rejoin his Mother who relaxed in comfort by lying across the leather settee. Jenny luxuriated in a position of comfort.

Michael stood in front of his Mother who was comfortable, lying down on the settee gracefully. Her legs were graceful.

"Mom. Didn't you get enough sleep?" asked son.

"I couldn't sleep. Gosh! I woke up. And where was I? I found myself all alone in bed."

Michael was amused at his Mother. He laughed at his Mother.

"Mom. You're funny. You know that you're divorced."

Jenny enjoyed her restful relaxation for about another half an hour.

Michael sat down in the armchair. Everything was quite different now. There were current changes to their circumstances. It was peaceful at Christmastime. Today there was peace and quiet at Christmas.

Michael relaxed, sitting in an armchair. He felt enthralled at the seasonal joyousness. He was enchanted by the dark evening.

Michael stayed in the lounge whilst his Mother cooked in the kitchen. During the course of the evening, Mother and son sat together at the Dining table. They both ate their nice dinner. Also, they both drank a glassful of dry wine. Normally, Michael didn't drink wine but today at Christmas was an exception. He decided to enjoy the treat of it. Michael felt joyful, cheerful and happy. He took joy in the pleasure of Christmas!

During the rest of Christmas night time, Michael enjoyed the company of his Mother. He relaxed with his Mother in her presence in front of a fire while he engaged in a conversation with her. That Christmas night, Jenny gave her son her Bible to read. The Mother forced her son to read the scriptures. The son obeyed his Mother according to her wishes.

The next day, Michael stayed at home. He continued to watch Detective Films on television, continually being shown every day during the morning.

Many hours later, Michael watched another film. Michael was a film buff. On the same day, he wrote out his remaining Christmas cards and posted them in a postbox just before the last collection.

On another day he went to his Aunt's house. He had been invited for dinner. He spent time with his spoilt Niece. He ended up spending the night at his Aunt's house.

On Christmas Eve, Michael and his Mother went Christmas shopping in a local shopping centre. It was late-night shopping. At a retail outlet, Michael bought new clothes from a clothes shop and Department Store in the shopping centre. They also bought food shopping from a supermarket. At that time it was crowded with Christmas shoppers shopping.

Arriving home, Michael and his Mother lounged by the fire. Keeping warm. They both ate and drank. They both relaxed together at Christmas. Son and Mother had a Christmas conversation.

The lounge itself looked Christmassy with Christmas decorations decorating. This particular Christmas was wonderful and the aura too. It was a marvellous experience with son and Mother both alone together on Christmas Eve.

The peace of Christmas (Eve) was so precious. It was an unforgettable Christmas! It lived on in their Christmas memories. From their beautiful Christmas experience, they both felt such bliss, joy and ecstasy at Christmas.

Chapter 4:

Christmas Day

On Christmas Day, Michael and his Mother attended a Christmas Sunday Service at a Chapel.

The congregation and choirboys by the choir sang hymns and Christmas carols. Michael and his Mother sat in a position at the far corner of an aisle near the clerestory. The Clergyman standing at the pulpit gave a sermon about the true significance of Christmas. The Nativity as well as the true Christian values of Christmas.

Michael felt enlightened and illuminated from listening to the sermon and prophesy.

Getting back home, Michael rested in bed. Having recovered from resting, in his bedroom Michael relaxed all alone. He played his favourite Artist. Listening to the bravura and music itself, lyrics and Artist. Michael had inspirational wonder. This particular Artist was a divine inspiration. The Artist was so magnificent.

Sometime in the mid-afternoon, Michael and his Mother had a Christmas dinner. His Mother had a roast. He had a vegetarian meal. This treat at Christmas made such a nice difference. They both indulged in a glass of sweet wine. Mother and son toasted together.

"Merry Christmas!"

Mother and son remained puritanical at Christmas. Hours earlier they opened their Christmas presents under a Christmas Tree.

Michael seemed utterly dissatisfied with his Christmas presents. His Mother received good Christmas gifts.

Neither of them was watching television on Christmas Day at this time.

Mother and son stayed together and talked away into the late hours of Christmas night. They both had a philosophical conversation. Jenny remained puritanical, philosophised. His sober Mother was experienced about one's life!

Chapter 5:

Boxing Day

On Boxing Day, Mrs Brewer cooked for Jenny and her son at Jenny's house. Mrs Brewer was a professional cook, a Gourmet. The cook took the time and made a lasagne according to Jenny's request.

At the Dining table, Jenny and her son ate a vegetarian lasagne. With it, they drank a glass of white wine.

Mrs Brewer stood at the Dining table watching them both eat their delicious vegetarian dish. They both gourmandised and drank.

"Do you like it?" asked Mrs Brewer.

"It's delicious," replied Jenny.

"Oh! Yeah. Love it. It's scrummy," remarked Michael.

"I am glad you like it. Everybody loves my cooking," said Mrs Brewer modestly.

"Do they. Tell me. Who have you cooked for?" wondered Michael.

"I have cooked at Girls' schools. The Girls just love my cooking," replied Mrs Brewer.

From this surprise, Michael became deeply impassioned.

"Do they really!"

Michael cherished his precious time with Mrs Brewer. The professional cook.

According to Michael, it remained an unforgettable deep memory of his.

Chapter 6:

On a Christmas Morning

On another morning, Michael continued to watch the Detective Season on television. Of course, he had a passion for those Nostalgic Films. He preferred the nostalgia. Certainly, a personal favourite. A black and white classic.

Michael stayed indoors and watched films day and night. He was aware of the Film Certificates of these films which made him choose carefully certain ones which he wanted to watch.

At Christmastime, he went to a family house. He had been invited. During those particular hours, he had been neglected by his family members. Michael at Christmas felt unhappy and miserable. There he met strangers. None of his family bothered to introduce them to him. They didn't introduce them to him. The few strangers had left when he arrived. Other members of his family gained more attention and favouritism. Since Michael had been invited, he fulfilled his obligational intention to come and see all his family at Christmas.

That Christmas afternoon with the family he ate a Christmas dinner. His family celebrated Christmas together. The merry revellers toasted each other.

Michael felt uncomfortable, miserable and unhappy and left his family after about a few hours. He had no wish to return. Coming and seeing his family members at their homes remained a Christmas misery. He felt quite melancholic, depressed and moody. Suffering from unhappy moody depression.

Going to his cousin's house at Christmas, his cousin showed him all of his many Christmas presents. Michael envied how his cousin received quality gifts. He had only received cheap gifts. In preference, his family showed favouritism towards his cousin.

His cousin was proud of himself. His cousin wore English cricket gear. His stance was that of a Batsman. Holding a cricket bat for batting.

"A batty man," said Michael humorously.

Michael was jealous of his cousin because he belonged to a cricket club.

Feeling envious, Michael left his cousin's house. Due to intrusion on his privacy. For Michael, it was another poor Christmas!

During the course of the Christmas week, during the last week of Christmas, Michael enjoyed his enjoyable seasonal Christmas experience alone with his beloved Mother. Those actual Christmas days alone with his beloved Mother were a pleasurable Christmas joy!

Invitation to the Family

On 28th December, Michael had been invited to his family's cosy house; his extended family. There at their home, Michael played board games with his relatives. They each played different board games in a living room with a fireplace in it. The room was warmed up by a fire.

Michael played a whodunnit game. He did not know how to play it. His player was rather good at this game. The others played games of chess, draughts and solitaire.

At this Christmastime, the day was rather different from all the other days.

Michael enjoyed playing a hard board game. He actually enjoyed the Christmas spirit of fun. He relaxed in the lovely warmth of the room. The warm temperature felt pleasantly warm and nice. He was enchanted by the enchantment of the firelight flickering and also the Christmassy beauty of the wooden room. A wooden interior.

On a day at Christmas, Michael spent time with his family. It was a joyful Christmas seasonal experience. To Michael it was a Christmas memory.

New Year's Celebration

On New Year's Eve, Michael stayed indoors. He felt lonely that New Year's Eve Day. Staying up late at night in his bedroom. His Mother burst into his bedroom.

"Come, son. They're here. Come join us for a drink," said Mother cheerfully.

Michael and his Mother went downstairs. Entering a room, they both joined their Merry Families for a New Year's Day celebration.

At midnight, all of the revellers and merry-makers standing made a toast, celebrating the New Year.

"Happy New Year!" they exclaimed merrily.

Footnote

The Beginning of it.

A CHRISTMAS CONVERSATION OVER THE CHRISTMASES.

Michael had a deep contemplation of Christmas. A reflection on Christmas. Did Michael have a devotion to the Lord?

By being converted and devoted!

- THE END -

*Available worldwide from
Amazon and all good bookstores*

www.mtp.agency

www.facebook.com/mtp.agency

@mtp_agency

www.ingramcontent.com/pod-product-compliance
Lightning Source LLC
LaVergne TN
LVHW051218070526
838200LV00063B/4952